INTEGRITY RISKS AND RED FLAGS IN
HEALTH PROJECTS

JANUARY 2023

ASIAN DEVELOPMENT BANK

ISBN 978-92-9269-998-7 (print); 978-92-9269-999-4 (electronic)
Publication Stock No. SGP220604-2
DOI: http://dx.doi.org/10.22617/SGP220604-2

The views expressed in this publication are those of the authors and do not necessarily reflect
the views and policies of the Asian Development Bank (ADB) or its Board of Governors or
the governments they represent.

ADB does not guarantee the accuracy of the data included in this publication and accepts no
responsibility for any consequence of their use. The mention of specific companies or products
of manufacturers does not imply that they are endorsed or recommended by ADB in preference to
others of a similar nature that are not mentioned.

By making any designation of or reference to a particular territory or geographic area, or by using
the term "country" in this publication, ADB does not intend to make any judgments as to the legal
or other status of any territory or area.

Please contact pubsmarketing@adb.org if you have questions or comments with respect to
content, or if you wish to obtain copyright permission for your intended use that does not fall within
these terms, or for permission to use the ADB logo.

Corrigenda to ADB publications may be found at http://www.adb.org/publications/corrigenda.

Notes:
References in this publication to bidders, bids, bid evaluation committees, and bid evaluation
reports are used within the context of the procurement of works (contractors), goods (suppliers),
and consulting and non-consulting services.

All photos by ADB except when otherwise stated.

In this publication, "$" refers to United States dollars.

On the cover: **Primary healthcare in Mongolia**. A doctor attends to a patient at a modern clinic in
Zuunmod, Töv Province in Mongolia, where ADB's Third Health Sector Development Project aims
to improve primary healthcare throughout the country (photo by ADB).

Cover design by Paolo Tan.

CONTENTS

TABLES, FIGURE, BOXES, AND CHECKLISTS

FOREWORD

Since 2003, the Asian Development Bank's Office of Anticorruption and Integrity has conducted proactive integrity reviews (PIRs) to identify and address control weaknesses that give rise to integrity risks in ongoing sovereign operations. Insights from these PIRs are published in this series, *Integrity Risks and Red Flags*.

This publication highlights weaknesses and red flags identified through PIRs of seven health projects financed by ADB. Further volumes in the series feature insights from five other sectors: agriculture, natural resources, and rural development; education; energy; transport; and water. Through this sector-based series, governments, public bodies, and stakeholders engaged in designing and implementing projects can learn from past vulnerabilities and establish processes and controls to effectively mitigate integrity risks.

To help foster and sustain economic growth, ADB's Strategy 2030 underscores the strengthening of governance and institutional capacity as an operational priority in the bank's developing member countries. Let us achieve a prosperous, inclusive, resilient, and sustainable Asia and the Pacific by maintaining the highest ethical standards.

John Versantvoort
Head, Office of Anticorruption and Integrity
Asian Development Bank

ACKNOWLEDGMENTS

Integrity Risks and Red Flags in Health Projects was prepared and developed collaboratively by H. Lorraine Wang (former advisor), Caridad Garrido Ortega (consultant and former senior integrity specialist), and Erickson Quijano (consultant) of the Preventive and Compliance Division, Office of Anticorruption and Integrity, Asian Development Bank.

This publication greatly benefited from the insights and comments of John Versantvoort (head), David Binns (former advisor), Lisa Kelaart-Courtney (director), Jung Min Han (senior integrity specialist), and Kristopher Marasigan (integrity officer) of the Office of Anticorruption and Integrity. This publication was made possible by the reviews from Rachana Shrestha (public management specialist, Sustainable Development and Climate Change Department) and Alaysa Escandor (public management officer - Governance, Sustainable Development and Climate Change Department).

ABBREVIATIONS

ADB	Asian Development Bank
BEC	bid evaluation committee
BER	bid evaluation report
OAI	Office of Anticorruption and Integrity
PIR	proactive integrity review
PMU	project management unit

INTRODUCTION

Since the Asian Development Bank (ADB) adopted its Anticorruption Policy in 1998, fighting corruption has become embedded in ADB's broader work in governance, public administration, and capacity development.[1] The Anticorruption Policy affirms the bank's zero tolerance for corruption and lays the groundwork for supporting anticorruption efforts.

ADB's Strategy 2030 identifies strengthening governance and institutional capacity as one of seven operational priorities for a prosperous, inclusive, resilient, and sustainable Asia and the Pacific. The Office of Anticorruption and Integrity (OAI) promotes the implementation of this operational priority through a combination of activities aimed at (i) enforcement and (ii) prevention and compliance.

The proactive integrity review (PIR) is a mechanism used by ADB since 2003 to help prevent and detect integrity violations and address risks in ADB-financed or -administered projects. PIRs (i) identify and assess integrity risks in procurement, contract and asset management, and financial management of a project; and (ii) recommend measures to mitigate these risks to ensure that project funds are used for their intended purposes.

PIRs evaluate the adherence of projects to three core principles of project integrity: (i) transparency—proper documentation of key decisions, public disclosure of project information, and protection of confidential information; (ii) fairness—objective and reliable bidding process and requirements optimizing competition, impartial evaluation, and a credible complaints mechanism; and (iii) accountability and control—accurate and timely project accounting and reporting, eligibility of expenditures and timely payments, adherence to contract provisions, and adequate project oversight and management.

OAI ensures that PIR knowledge is applied to the projects reviewed through follow-up reviews, at which time OAI verifies the implementation status of the PIR. In addition, OAI assists the executing and implementing agencies in addressing open recommendations.[2]

PIR knowledge is institutionalized in ADB operations through (i) embedding of PIR requirements in ADB guidance and instruction documents, (ii) integrity risk management reviews, (iii) knowledge enhancement and transfer workshops and other learning courses, and (iv) knowledge products.[3] Following a country-focused approach (one of three guiding principles outlined in Strategy 2030), PIR knowledge also informs the country partnership strategies of developing member countries (DMCs).[4] Through this exercise, PIR knowledge is considered in designing new projects as the country partnership strategy predominantly drives country operations business plans.

This publication presents vulnerabilities from PIRs of seven health projects (Appendix) across five countries and three regions and highlights recommended measures to mitigate identified integrity risks.[5]

---

[1] ADB. 1998. *Anticorruption Policy*. Manila.

[2] The follow-up review reports document the implementation status of PIR recommendations (footnote 5).

[3] Through integrity risk management reviews, PIR knowledge is built in preapproval project documents (concept papers, reports and recommendations of the President to the Board of Directors, technical assistance reports).

[4] The country partnership strategy is the primary platform for defining ADB's operational focus in a developing member country.

[5] The health projects reviewed were selected from all active ADB-financed loan and grant projects using a risk-based selection process. The selection process took into account the size of funding, lending modality, implementation arrangements, number of awarded contracts, level of disbursements, input from relevant ADB departments, prior project results, external benchmarking, and potential benefits of a proactive integrity review (PIR) to the project. PIR reports are available on the ADB website (https://www.adb.org/who-we-are/integrity/proactive-integrity-review).

SECTOR OVERVIEW

ADB launched the Operational Plan for Health 2015–2020 in June 2015. The plan describes how ADB will support DMCs in achieving universal health coverage. Key priorities are investing in health infrastructure, health governance, and financing; all underpinned by investments in information and communication technology and public–private partnerships.

Table 1 presents the financial resources commitments by ADB in the health sector from 2017 to 2021.

Table 1: ADB's Financing Commitments in the Health Sector, 2017–2021

YEAR	2017	2018	2019	2020	2021
Value ($ million)	219	524	644	3,512	5,882
Percent of commitments in all sectors	1.01%	2.14%	2.68%	11.12%	25.84%

Source: ADB. 2022. ADB Annual Report 2021. Manila.

INTEGRITY RISKS AND RED FLAGS

Methodology

OAI identified and synthesized integrity-related vulnerabilities, including red flags, from all its health PIR findings.[6] A vulnerability is any gap in a project's implementation processes that, if not remediated in a timely manner, will increase the likelihood of an integrity violation occurring and/or the impact of an integrity violation. In other words, the vulnerability increases the risk profile of the project.

Integrity risk is the risk that project funds are diverted from their intended purposes due to fraud, corruption, and other integrity violations.[7] Integrity violations are more likely to occur if integrity risks are not identified and addressed effectively and in a timely manner. Integrity risk management is an essential prerequisite for ensuring that projects achieve the intended development outcomes.

OAI also assessed the level of vulnerabilities (high, medium, or low) by occurrence and impact.[8] This publication follows the project implementation processes and related subprocesses shown in Table 2. It also discusses high- and medium-risk vulnerabilities and mitigating measures in each project implementation process.

Table 2: Project Implementation Processes

Process			
Procurement	**Contract and Asset Management**	**Financial Management**

Subprocess		
A1 Bidding Prequalification, bidding documents preparation, bid advertisements, submissions, and opening	**B1 Contract administration** The management of the day-to-day practicalities and administrative requirements under the contract	**C1 Expenditure management** Approval and processing of payments for project expenditures
A2 Bid evaluation Assessment of bidders' compliance with bidding requirements, and preparation and approval of evaluation report	**B2 Output monitoring** Engagement with/supervision of contractors, consultants, and suppliers in relation to project outputs	**C2 Financial reporting** Project accounting and auditing
A3 Contract award Post-bid evaluation activities until contract is awarded and signed	**B3 Asset control** Safeguarding and maintenance of project assets including asset inventory	

Note: The subprocesses reflect those prioritized by the Office of Anticorruption and Integrity and do not reflect all subprocesses that exist within each process.
Source: Office of Anticorruption and Integrity, Asian Development Bank.

---

[6] Red flags are indicators of irregularities, which may indicate the occurrence of integrity violations. Project staff should be alert to red flags of integrity violations and promptly report potential violations to the OAI.

[7] Integrity violation is any act which violates ADB's Anticorruption Policy, including corrupt, fraudulent, coercive, or collusive practice; abuse; conflict of interest; obstructive practice; violations of ADB sanctions; retaliation against whistleblowers and witnesses; and others, including failure to adhere to the highest ethical standards.

[8] OAI determined the occurrence of a vulnerability by establishing the frequency with which this was identified in the PIRs; and based the impact of a vulnerability on the likelihood that this could have resulted in an integrity violation or misuse of project funds.

Integrity Risk Heat Maps

The heat map in Figure (a) shows the level of risk arising from vulnerabilities identified in health PIRs and presented in the processes in which they manifested. In the seven health projects reviewed, OAI identified high integrity risks in the procurement and contract and asset management processes.

Figure (b) shows the risk level by subprocess. Risk levels are highest in bidding (A1) and bid evaluation (A2) subprocesses.

Figure: Integrity Risk Heat Maps

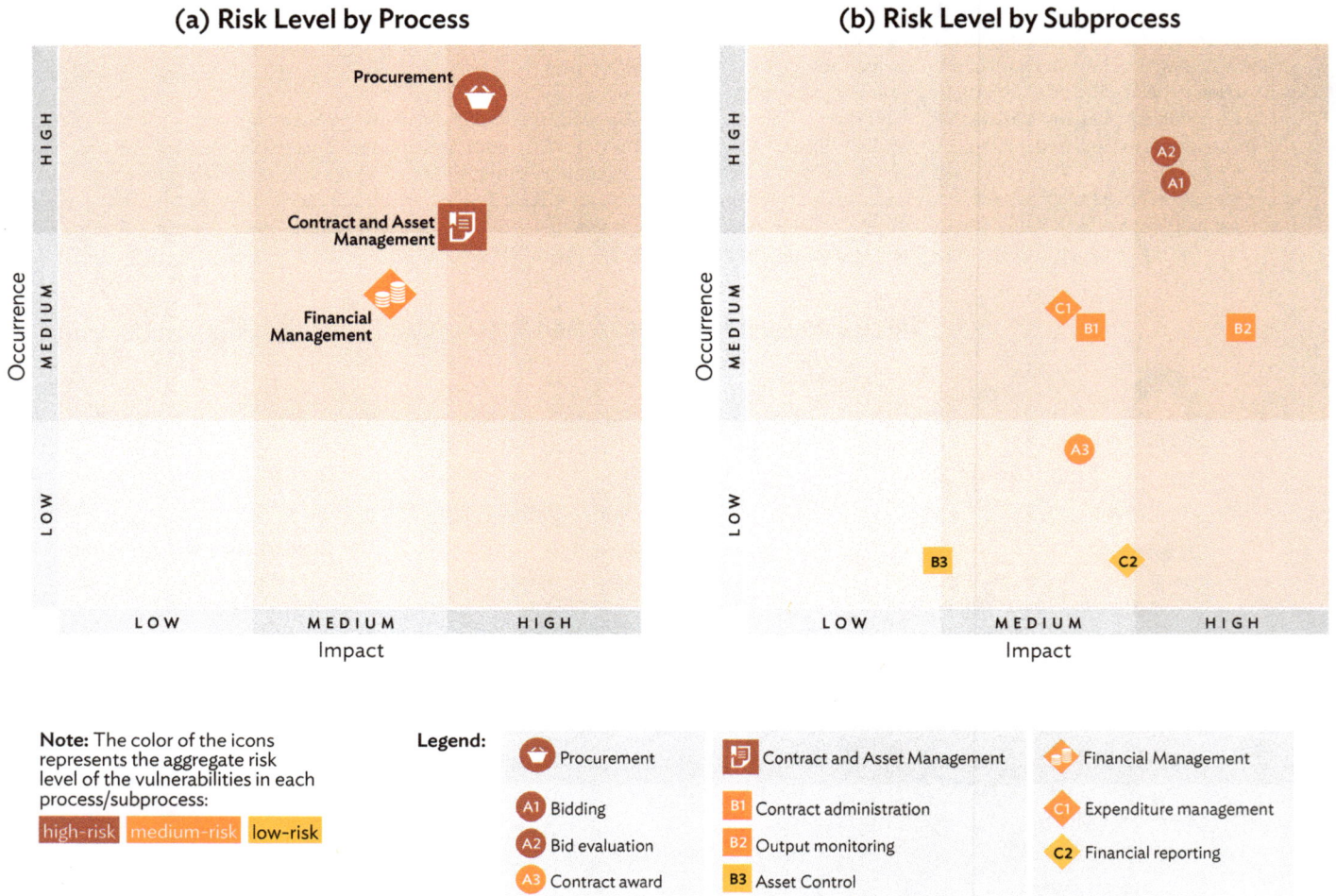

(a) Risk Level by Process

(b) Risk Level by Subprocess

Note: The color of the icons represents the aggregate risk level of the vulnerabilities in each process/subprocess: high-risk, medium-risk, low-risk

Legend:

- Procurement
- A1 Bidding
- A2 Bid evaluation
- A3 Contract award
- Contract and Asset Management
- B1 Contract administration
- B2 Output monitoring
- B3 Asset Control
- Financial Management
- C1 Expenditure management
- C2 Financial reporting

Source: Office of Anticorruption and Integrity, Asian Development Bank.

9   The heat map is a visual representation of relationships among two sets of data: the likelihood that an integrity violation may occur (occurrence) and its potential impact to the project (impact).

Vulnerabilities and Mitigating Measures

OAI's analysis aimed to identify factors contributing to integrity vulnerabilities and to formulate risk-mitigating measures. These measures may be applied to all projects regardless of their financing modality or structure. Project teams can use the due diligence checklists during bid evaluation (Checklist 1) and expenditure payment processing (Checklist 2) to identify and mitigate integrity risks.[10]

PROCUREMENT

(A1) Bidding

Red flags of integrity violations. OAI identified red flags that may have undermined the fairness of the bidding process. These may increase the likelihood of fraud and corruption, thereby jeopardizing the project. It may also give rise to alienating prospective bidders. Examples of red flags in bidding are summarized in Table 3.

Red flags are multifaceted, and those summarized in Table 3 may have one or a combination of the elements of collusion, fraud, corruption, and/or conflicts of interest.

Table 3: Examples of Red Flags in Bidding

Type of Integrity Violation	Red Flags
Collusive practice	**Similarities in bids** • Bids had the same formatting, specifications, and language. • Bidders proposed the same brand and country of origin for the proposed common items, and made the same typographical errors. • Some documents in a bid appeared to be photocopies of documents in another bid. **Apparent connections between bidders** • Bidders had the same addresses and/or telephone numbers. • A bidder's company stamp appeared in the other bidder's documents. The same bidder certified and signed some of the other bidders' documents. • Bidders had common major shareholders. **Allowing unreasonably short time to respond to requests for bids** Bidders were only given half of the minimum number of days required by the national procurement law to prepare and submit bids. Also, the deadlines for the sale of bidding documents were on the same day as the bid opening. This could have restricted fair competition, which resulted in the project management unit receiving only one to two bids in four procurements, and significant delays in the completion of three contracts. **Unusual bid patterns** • Bid prices of winning and losing bidders were similar in 19 out of 42 contracts reviewed. • Bid securities submitted by bidders had sequential numbers.
Corrupt practice	**Unjustified high prices** Price of assets significantly exceeded the market prices for 24 (44%) out of 54 reviewed contracts, with the excess in price ranging from 20% to 195%. Assets include medical equipment, laboratory equipment, computers, software, and data processors, and incompatible contract pricing was due to the owner's incorrect or unjustified estimates.

Notes: 1. Collusive practice is an arrangement between two or more parties designed to achieve an improper purpose, including influencing improperly the actions of another party.
2. Corrupt practice is the offering, giving, receiving, or soliciting, directly or indirectly, anything of value to influence improperly the actions of another party.
Source: Office of Anticorruption and Integrity, Asian Development Bank.

---

[10] OAI rolled out project management checklists to help executing and implementing agencies to self-assess (i) executing/implementing agency capacity, (ii) project procurement processes, (iii) financial management, and (iv) project output management from an integrity perspective. These checklists are available at https://www.adb.org/who-we-are/integrity/proactive-integrity-review.

🔧 **MITIGATING MEASURES**
Red Flags of Integrity Violations

- ADB regional departments and resident missions should ensure that executing and/or implementing agencies, including project implementing units or offices and evaluation committees, understand their obligations under ADB's Anticorruption Policy, especially the obligation to report any integrity violation to OAI when such allegation is initially identified or suspected. Executing and/or implementing agencies should communicate these obligations to the bidders (contractors, consultants, suppliers); provide the necessary oversight; and

conduct appropriate due diligence to minimize the risk of integrity violations on development projects.

- The executing agency should exercise tighter oversight on the implementing agency and preclude conflicts of interest with project officials. The executing agency should (i) establish a mechanism to identify and manage perceived or actual conflicts of interest, which might include requiring implementing agency staff to disclose their relationships with contractors/consultants/suppliers; and (ii) actively monitor its staff integrity and require them to adhere to the highest ethical standards.

Deficient and inconsistent information in the bidding documents. Without clear and consistent requirements in the bidding documents, bid evaluation may become subjective and prone to errors. If not mitigated, evaluation errors may lead to the selection of unqualified bidders, thereby exposing the project to losses. Two examples of this vulnerability are summarized in Table 4.

Table 4: Examples of Deficient and Inconsistent Information in the Bidding Documents

Bid Requirement	Nature of Deficient/Inconsistent Information
Materials specifications	Indeterminate terms such as "best quality," "superior quality," "foreign made," and "locally made" were used to described specifications of required materials in the bidding documents. These terms are not specific enough to determine the quality standards to be applied to materials, and make it difficult to seek recourse if substandard materials were used. ⚠️
Financial position	One section of the bidding documents stated that financial position would be assessed based on the audited financial statements (i.e., net worth). However, another section prescribed assessment of financial position based on the existence of debts.

Legend: ⚠️ = indicative of rigged specifications (collusive practice). Collusive practice is an arrangement between two or more parties designed to achieve an improper purpose, including influencing improperly the actions of another party.
Source: Office of Anticorruption and Integrity, Asian Development Bank.

🔧 **MITIGATING MEASURES**
Deficient and Inconsistent Information in the Bidding Documents

- The executing and/or implementing agencies should (i) refer to ADB's guidance notes on procurement during the preparation of the bidding documents and (ii) provide clear and consistent information in the bidding documents to enable bidders to prepare responsive bids.

- The regional departments should (i) thoroughly review the draft bidding documents submitted by executing and/or implementing agencies to ensure accuracy of required information and (ii) report any potential integrity violation to OAI when such is initially identified or suspected.

(A2) Bid Evaluation

Vulnerabilities in bid evaluation can result in contracts awarded to unqualified bidders, thereby undermining the transparency and fairness of the procurement at an ultimate cost to the project. Process inconsistencies and deficiencies, and inaccurate evaluation results may create the impression of favoring bidders. If not addressed, these vulnerabilities may eventually lead to substandard outputs, delayed implementation, waste, loss of funds, or harm to the intended beneficiaries.

Inadequate due diligence. Bidders may provide dubious information on their eligibility, financial capacity, and experience. Without adequate due diligence during bid evaluation, the bid evaluation committees (BECs) may fail to identify irregularities, inconsistencies, and/or potential misrepresentation.

Following a risk-based approach, the BEC should conduct due diligence to verify the submitted bid information against supporting documents (records check), from online sources (sanctions and other desktop research including previous adverse news), and/or from third parties (reference check). Combined with professional attributes such as a questioning mind and a critical assessment of documents, due diligence requires looking for indications of errors and/or misrepresentations on the documents, including checking the accuracy of information drawn from computations. The BEC should also seek clarifications and/or substantiation from bidders to the extent allowed by the bidding documents.

Examples of these evaluation errors resulting from the lack of, or inadequate due diligence are summarized in Table 5. Box 1 presents sample cases of bid evaluation errors.

Table 5: Examples of Evaluation Errors

Bid Evaluation Aspect/ Requirement	Nature of Evaluation Error
Financial capacity	• A winning bidder submitted certifications issued by financial institutions that it had no outstanding debts, yet the bidder's financial statements showed a balance for liabilities. The bidder explained that the liabilities were advances for ongoing contracts. However, the executing agency did not verify the bidder's explanation with the creditors (for the advances) nor with the financial institutions. • The financial statements included in the bid were not the same statements submitted to the tax authority. ⚠️ Ⓐ
Conflict of interest	The consultant selection committee did not identify the potential conflict of interest in one of the winning consulting firm's nominated experts who was a current employee of the executing agency at the time of bidding. ⚠️ Ⓐ
Past poor performance	A bidder was awarded a contract despite not having met warranty and maintenance obligations in a previous contract. Consequently, the project suffered delays. Ⓑ
Experience	**Goods** The bid evaluation committee incorrectly assessed the bidders' contractual experience due to incorrect formula and exchange rates used. The assessment was corrected only after a losing bidder raised a complaint. **Works** • The bid evaluation committee based its evaluation of experience only on the bidder's submitted list of construction works, where some declared projects could not be traced to the submitted proof of completed works. • The total value of a bidder's completed works in the list it submitted was higher than the reported construction revenues in the audited financial statements. ⚠️ Ⓐ

Legend: ⚠️ = indicative of potential integrity violation.

Ⓐ = Indicative of potential misrepresentation (fraudulent practice). Fraudulent practice is any act or omission, including a misrepresentation, that knowingly or recklessly misleads, or attempts to mislead, a party to obtain a financial or other benefit or to avoid an obligation.

Ⓑ = Indicative of potential bribery, i.e., questionable, improper, or repeated selection of a particular contractor because of bribes (corrupt practice). Corrupt practice is the offering, giving, receiving, or soliciting, directly or indirectly, anything of value to influence improperly the actions of another party.

Source: Office of Anticorruption and Integrity, Asian Development Bank.

PROCUREMENT

CONTRACT
AND ASSET
MANAGEMENT

FINANCIAL
MANAGEMENT

OTHER
VULNERABILITIES

Box 1: Cases—Bid Evaluation Errors

Case 1: Conflict of Interest

One of the winning consultant's nominated experts was a current employee of the project's executing agency at the time of proposal submission. Based on the personnel evaluation sheet, the consultant selection committee did not recognize the potential conflict of interest and still evaluated the expert's qualifications. The consultant selection committee should have identified the potential conflict of interest and assigned a zero rating to the position. The said expert was eventually replaced as the executing agency requested for a replacement during contract negotiations. However, the executing agency replaced the expert due to the expert's unsatisfactory rating, and not because of conflict of interest.

CASE 1 TAKEAWAY

Check for conflicts of interest to ensure that the consulting firm and/or its experts are not subject to actual or potential conflict that impacts their capacity to serve the best interest of the executing agency.

The consulting firm and/or its experts are required to provide professional, objective, and impartial advice, at all times holding the executing agency's interests paramount, strictly avoiding conflicts with other assignments or their own corporate and personal interests, and acting without any consideration for future work.

Case 2: Experience—Incorrect Computation and Use of Exchange Rates

The bid evaluation committee (BEC) incorrectly evaluated bidders' compliance with the contractual experience criteria due to incorrect treatment of two items:

(i) The BEC compared the combined value of all completed contracts against the required minimum contract amount, instead of checking whether each contract met or exceeded the minimum threshold amount.

(ii) The BEC erroneously converted contracts completed in prior periods using the exchange rate as of the bid opening date, not the average exchange rate in the year the contract was completed (based on generally accepted accounting principles).

A complaint from a losing bidder prompted the BEC to revisit its procedures and revise the evaluation by comparing the individual dollar values of the winning bidder's two contracts against the minimum required contract amount. However, the BEC used an incorrect exchange rate to recompute the contract amounts. Based on this incorrect reevaluation, the winning bidder did not meet the minimum required value. Without other qualified bidders, the BEC recommended a rebidding.

The rebidding prompted the winning bidder to complain that the rebidding was inappropriate. This complaint led the finance ministry to review the BEC's evaluation, which noted the incorrect exchange rate used to convert the winning bidder's contracts. Based on the reevaluation, the winning bidder met the contractual experience criteria.

CASE 2 TAKEAWAY

Bid evaluation errors undermine the fairness of the procurement and waste resources. Procurement inefficiencies (e.g., rebidding) could have been avoided had the BEC performed control checks on the computational aspects of the evaluation.

Source: Office of Anticorruption and Integrity, Asian Development Bank.

Inconsistent application of bid evaluation criteria. This may give the perception of favoritism or undue influence. Examples of inconsistent application of bid evaluation criteria are summarized in Table 6.

Table 6: Examples of Inconsistent Application of Bid Evaluation Criteria

Bid Evaluation Aspect/Requirement	Nature of Inconsistent Application of Bid Evaluation Criteria
Average sales requirement	There were inconsistencies in the treatment of the average sales requirement during the evaluation of bids (e.g., both initial and reevaluation) for a procurement package. The "new" winning bidder determined after reevaluation was previously disqualified in the initial evaluation for not meeting the average sales requirement. On the other hand, the winning bidder declared during the initial evaluation (losing bidder after reevaluation) was disqualified in the reevaluation because it did not meet the average sales requirement.
International experience	National experts with valid international experience were incorrectly rated (given a zero score), while others with no international experience were given a score above zero. ⚠

⚠ = indicative of bid manipulation (collusive practice). Collusive practice is an arrangement between two or more parties designed to achieve an improper purpose, including influencing improperly the actions of another party.
Source: Office of Anticorruption and Integrity, Asian Development Bank.

Incomplete information in bid evaluation reports. Inadequate and unclear information in bid evaluation reports (BERs) may appear to conceal erroneous or subjective assessments, thereby favoring certain bidders. Examples of incomplete information in BERs are summarized in Table 7.

Table 7: Examples of Incomplete Information in the Bid Evaluation Reports

Bid Evaluation Report Item	Nature of Incomplete Information in the Bid Evaluation Reports
All criteria	The bid evaluation report (BER) did not include a detailed evaluation matrix nor information on how each of the criteria was assessed. The BER showed comparisons of bidders' proposed prices, but did not include any reference to other evaluation and qualification criteria.
Technical experience	The BER neither presented the results of evaluation of technical experience of bidders nor explained the reasons for not considering the bidders' technical experience during bid evaluation. Thus, it appeared that the bid evaluation committee (BEC) did not evaluate the technical experience of the bidders, which is one of the major evaluation criteria.
Signatures of BEC members	The BEC members did not sign the BER and minutes of BEC meetings.

Source: Office of Anticorruption and Integrity, Asian Development Bank.

Absence of documentation to support bid evaluation decisions. The lack of documented BEC decisions in the bidding process diminishes the transparency and fairness of the bid evaluation process. Examples of bid evaluation documentation deficiencies are in Table 8.

Table 8: Examples of Bid Evaluation Documentation Deficiencies

Bidding Requirement	Nature of Bid Evaluation Documentation Deficiency
Proposed experts' qualifications	There were no guidelines nor scoring approach to guide the bid evaluation committee assessment of the evaluation criteria (general qualifications, project-related experience, and country experience) and allocation of scores for each sub-criterion during the evaluation of proposed experts' qualifications.
Technical experience	It was unclear how the bid evaluation committee assessed the bidders' technical experience since the submitted bids did not contain adequate information to complete a thorough assessment. Clarifications were also not sought from all the bidders to bridge information gaps.

Source: Office of Anticorruption and Integrity, Asian Development Bank.

PROCUREMENT

CONTRACT
AND ASSET
MANAGEMENT

FINANCIAL
MANAGEMENT

OTHER
VULNERABILITIES

MITIGATING MEASURES
Vulnerabilities in Bid Evaluation

- BEC members should undergo detailed and practical hands-on training on all aspects of bid evaluation, especially due diligence, before undertaking new bid evaluation assignments. Support from ADB regional departments, supervision consultants, and engaged procurement experts is required (a checklist on how to avoid common errors/lapses in bid evaluation is on Checklist 1).

- ADB regional departments should perform rigorous reviews of BERs, particularly when the executing agency's procurement capacity is not robust or when contracts are high-value, high-risk, or complex. Rigorous review entails seeking clarifications from the executing and/or implementing agencies, calling in bids on a sample basis, validating evaluation report information against bids, and assessing the reasonableness of significant evaluation committee decisions.

- The executing and/or implementing agency should hold pre-bid meetings for high-value, high-risk, or complex procurements, where bidding requirements are carefully discussed with bidders. The BEC must consistently apply these requirements.

- The executing and/or implementing agency should check accuracy and completeness of information in BERs before submitting these for ADB's no-objection. For transparency, decisions made and justifications for deviations noted should be properly documented in the BERs.

Checklist 1: How to Avoid Common Errors and Lapses in Bid Evaluation

ADB Sanctions List
☐ Verify that the bidder (all parties to the joint venture/association/consortium agreement) is not on ADB's complete Sanctions List (https://sanctions.adb.org).

Construction Turnover
☐ Verify the turnover declared on the bidding form against the turnover reported in the audited financial statements submitted.

Financial Capacity
☐ Verify the financial capacity-related accounts (working capital, net worth) declared on the bidding form against the corresponding accounts in the audited financial statements submitted.

☐ Verify the credit lines declared against the supporting documents submitted.

Current Contract Commitments
☐ Verify the current contract commitments declared on the bidding form against the contract commitments reported in the audited financial statements submitted.

Experience
☐ Verify the experience declared in the bidding form against the work completion certificates (for works) and curricula vitae (for experts/consultants) submitted.

Pending Litigation
☐ Verify the pending litigations declared on the bidding form against the pending litigation disclosures in the audited financial statements submitted.

Criteria Requiring Computations
☐ Recompute the amounts on the bidding forms and verify that the formula used, including the exchange rates, are correct.

ADB = Asian Development Bank, OAI = Office of Anticorruption and Integrity.
Note: Where a red flag is identified, refer it to OAI for further verification.
Source: Office of Anticorruption and Integrity, Asian Development Bank.

(A3) Contract Award

Deficient performance securities. Deficient or delayed submission of performance securities results in inadequate protection to the executing agency in case of a contractor's or supplier's breach of contract. This heightens the risk of increased project cost and implementation delays. Examples of deficiencies in performance securities are as follows:

(i)   No records as evidence on the contractors' submission of the performance securities.

(ii) Performance securities submitted after contract signing.

(iii) Performance securities with amounts lower than the contract requirement.

(iv) Performance securities with validity dates ending before the goods were expected to be delivered and were not subsequently extended.

MITIGATING MEASURES
Deficient Performance Securities

The executing and/or implementing agencies should strictly enforce the performance security requirement. In cases of delay in the delivery of goods or completion of services, the contractor/supplier should be requested to appropriately extend the validity period of the performance security.

CONTRACT AND ASSET MANAGEMENT

B1 Contract Administration

Deficient insurance and warranties. Without adequate and valid securities, including insurance, the executing agency has no recourse if (i) project assets are damaged or lost (including injury or death of the workers); and (ii) the supplier/contractor does not fulfill its warranty obligations, thereby jeopardizing the ultimate beneficial goal of the project. Examples of insurance and warranty concerns are in Table 9.

Table 9: Examples of Insurance and Warranty Concerns

Item	Insurance/Warranty Concerns
Insurance on goods in transit	• A supplier did not provide insurance certificates after delivering the goods and requesting payment. • A supplier provided insurance coverage that expired before the goods were delivered at a designated warehouse. • Suppliers submitted invalid insurance certificates because these (i) did not contain the essential information (validity period of the insurance, name of the beneficiary/holder of the insurance certificate, description of goods insured); and (ii) were copies of the original certificates.
Insurance on construction works	A contractor did not provide the required insurance for loss of and/or damage to project assets and bodily injury to and/or death of workers.
Warranty letters	• The suppliers did not provide complete warranty letters to the end users (hospitals). • The warranty letters indicated a coverage of 1 year from the issuance of the final acceptance certificates. However, the final acceptance certificates did not indicate the acceptance dates, making it difficult to determine the start date of the warranty coverage. • The warranty letter for the quality of construction did not indicate the warranty period.

Source: Office of Anticorruption and Integrity, Asian Development Bank.

PROCUREMENT

**CONTRACT
AND ASSET
MANAGEMENT**

FINANCIAL
MANAGEMENT

OTHER
VULNERABILITIES

🔧 **MITIGATING MEASURES**
Deficient Insurance
and Warranties

- The executing and/or implementing agencies should obtain adequate insurance from suppliers, including the corresponding insurance certificates containing complete information in terms of validity period, correct beneficiary, and description of coverage.

In cases of delay in the delivery of goods or completion of services, the contractor/supplier should be requested to appropriately extend the validity period of the insurance.

- The executing and/or implementing agencies should require (i) the contractors/suppliers to provide the warranty certificates, with validity dates specified, to the end users; and (ii) end users to indicate the acceptance dates on the final acceptance certificates.

B2 Output Monitoring

Use of substandard materials and works that were substandard, defective, or off-specifications. Executing and implementing agencies should ensure that contractors and suppliers are adequately supervised and that any issues are addressed in a timely manner. The PIR asset inspection of health projects identified output defects, deviations from approved designs/specifications, and use of substandard materials which could have been detected and rectified earlier had the project supervision been more robust. This inadequate supervision of the entities executing the project activities resulted in delays, inferior quality of works, and cost overruns. An example of these issues is in Box 2.

Box 2: Case—Use of Substandard Materials and Substandard/Defective Works

Effect of Off-Specification Works on Medical Goods Purchased. The proactive integrity review inspection team noted that medical equipment representing 13% of the contract value installed at a hospital in one of the districts was not operational because the associated pipeline was improperly installed. Sixteen units of incinerators representing 68% of the contract value for various health centers in another district were not functional due to lack of electrical capacity. Project beneficiaries suffered as a result of accepting medical equipment that were not operational.

TAKEAWAY
The importance of project supervision during project implementation cannot be overemphasized. The defects noted above could have been detected and resolved at the onset had project supervision been vigorous.

🔧 **MITIGATING MEASURES**
Use of Substandard Materials and
Works That Were Substandard,
Defective, or Off-Specifications

- Erring contractors, consultants, and suppliers should be held accountable to ensure that they fulfill their contractual obligations. This entails enforcing the defects rectification and penalty clauses and reporting poor performance to ADB without delay.

- For decentralized, complex, or high-risk projects, independent third-party monitoring firms should be engaged to augment the monitoring activities performed by the executing and/or implementing agencies, ADB regional departments, and supervision consultants.

- Executing and/or implementing agencies should closely monitor the supervision consultants. This entails rigorous review of the consultants' progress reports and, as necessary, verification of progress through field visits. A guide that provides a practical framework for field visits/asset inspections can be accessed through this link: https://www.adb.org/sites/default/files/institutional-document/431571/asset-inspection-project-integrity.pdf.

FINANCIAL MANAGEMENT

C1 Expenditure Management

Ineligible expenditures. Executing/ implementing agencies should counter the risk of payments made for ineligible expenditures. Expenditures that are (i) not within the contract terms, (ii) inadequately or inappropriately supported, or (iii) unauthorized are considered ineligible. These indicate that claims were not thoroughly reviewed against contract provisions. They provide opportunities for fraud and expose the project to the risk of loss of funds. Examples of lapses in expenditure management are summarized in Table 10.

Table 10: Examples of Ineligible Expenditures

Expenditure Category	Lapse/Gap in the Expenditure
Goods	• There was no evidence that goods paid for were the specific items ordered and in good condition. Handover minutes documenting the transfer of goods from the PMU to the implementing agencies were used to substantiate payments to suppliers, rather than delivery notes that PMU received from suppliers. • Supporting documents to supplier invoices, such as bills of lading, packing lists, insurance certificates, warranty certificates, inspection certificates, and certificates of origin, were not attached to the invoices as required by the contract. • Goods delivered originated from countries that were different from the countries stated in the contract. One of the countries was not an ADB member.
Training expenses	• The PMU's internal documents were used to support processing of payments for training expenses. Third party-issued documents, such as bills from hotels and restaurants and invoices/receipts from supply stores, were not submitted. • The supporting budget request for training was approved despite the absence of a detailed breakdown or descriptions of the expense items.

ADB = Asian Development Bank, PMU = project management unit.
Source: Office of Anticorruption and Integrity, Asian Development Bank.

MITIGATING MEASURES
Ineligible Expenditures

• Executing/implementing agencies should ensure that prior to endorsing claims for payment (i) payment approval procedures are followed, (ii) supporting documents are checked for accuracy and completeness, and (iii) details in the claims are validated against the contracts and supporting documents. Payments should be refused or reduced in line with relevant contractual provisions for works

or services that were not performed or goods that were not delivered (a checklist on how to avoid common errors/lapses in expenditure payment processing is on Checklist 2).

• ADB regional departments and resident missions should ensure that executing and implementing agencies, including project implementing units/offices, understand their obligations under ADB's Anticorruption Policy, especially the obligation to report any integrity violations to OAI without delay when such allegations are initially identified or suspected.

PROCUREMENT

CONTRACT
AND ASSET
MANAGEMENT

**FINANCIAL
MANAGEMENT**

**OTHER
VULNERABILITES**

Checklist 2: How to Avoid Common Errors and Lapses in Expenditure Payment Processing

All Types

☐ Verify the claim against the milestone payment terms stipulated in the contract (including contract variations).

☐ Check whether the payment information indicated in the claim matches with the payment information in the contract.

☐ Identify any red flags on the supporting documents submitted, e.g., erasures, alterations, or other errors and ask for clarifications.

Works (Contractors)

☐ Verify the claim against interim payment certificates/certificates of completion. Check if there are claims on non-workdays (work on a weekend or holiday with no preapproval).

Services (Consultants)

☐ Verify the remuneration claim (for input-based contracts) against detailed timesheets submitted.

☐ Verify claims for reimbursable expenses against supporting documents as required in the contract (not applicable for full lump-sum contracts), including:
  ○ Travel costs—proof of travel (tickets, receipts, boarding passes);
  ○ Accommodation—proof of stay (hotel bills, invoices, receipts); and
  ○ Seminars and workshops—attendance sheets, invoices or receipts for workshop costs like venue and equipment rental and refreshments.

Goods (Suppliers)

☐ Verify the claim against sales invoice and delivery receipt/proof that goods have been delivered, inspected, accepted, and, as necessary, properly installed.

Note: Where a red flag is identified, refer it to OAI for further verification.
Source: Office of Anticorruption and Integrity, Asian Development Bank.

OTHER INTEGRITY-RELATED VULNERABILITIES THAT CUT ACROSS PROJECT IMPLEMENTATION PROCESSES

Integrity risks in project implementation principally result from capacity gaps of the executing and/or implementing agency—particularly in procurement, contract and asset management, financial management processes, and in maintaining project records.

D1 Records Management

Missing or disorganized key project documents and absence of suitable records management. Inaccurate or incomplete audit trail of project activities complicates the timely prevention and detection of integrity violations, noncompliance, and errors. Executing and/or implementing agencies should maintain an effective records management system that evidences their compliance with anticorruption, procurement, financial management, and other relevant guidelines.

**MITIGATING MEASURES
Records Management Issues**

Executing and/or implementing agencies should establish and maintain an effective system of records management to (i) facilitate records identification, validation, storage, and retrieval; (ii) improve accountability; (iii) drive timely detection of errors and irregularities; and (iv) prevent misplacement.

CONCLUSION

Through its proactive integrity reviews of seven health projects, ADB's Office of Anticorruption and Integrity identified vulnerabilities and red flags in (i) procurement, (ii) contract and asset management, and (iii) financial management processes. Key vulnerabilities are summarized in Table 11.

To manage related risks, ADB encourages project staff to apply the mitigating measures recommended in this publication and use the due diligence checklists for bid evaluation (Checklist 1) and expenditure payment processing (Checklist 2). Project staff must remain alert to red flags of integrity violations and report suspected violations to the Office of Anticorruption and Integrity.

Integrity risks are generally elevated in complex, decentralized projects (i.e., large-scale projects involving numerous project components, geographical locations, and implementing entities). These projects benefit from strong accountability and control mechanisms that clarify responsibilities at each implementation level (from the executing agency down to the last implementing unit), and from closer supervision by the executing agency and ADB. Integrity-related controls should be embedded in contracts, manuals, and other authoritative documents.

Under Operational Priority 7 of Strategy 2030, ADB has committed to support governments in their efforts to eradicate corruption and implement anticorruption measures in all its projects and programs. We trust that the insights compiled in this publication will contribute to these endeavors.

Table 11: High- and Medium-Risk Vulnerabilities in Health Projects and their Implications

Process	Subprocess	Vulnerability	Risk Implication
Procurement	**A1** **Bidding**	Red flags of collusion (among bidders and executing agencies) and corrupt practices	Conflicts of interest, and fraud and corruption, jeopardizing the project and alienating prospective bidders
		Deficient and inconsistent information in bidding documents	Subjective or incorrect evaluations resulting in contract awards to unqualified bidders
	A2 **Bid evaluation**	Inadequate due diligence, inconsistent application of bid evaluation criteria, incomplete information in bid evaluation reports, and absence of documentation to support bid evaluation decisions	Diminished transparency and fairness of the bidding process resulting in contract awards to unqualified bidders
	A3 **Contract award**	Deficient performance securities	Uncompensated delays and losses caused by erring contractors or suppliers
Contract and asset management	**B1** **Contract administration**	Deficient securities and insurance	Uncompensated losses caused by erring contractors or suppliers, and damages or losses on project assets
	B2 **Output monitoring**	Use of substandard materials and works that were substandard, defective, or off-specifications resulting from the inadequate monitoring of contractors by executing/implementing agencies and supervision consultants	Implementation delays, inferior quality of outputs, and cost overruns
Financial management	**C1** **Expenditure management**	Ineligible, unsupported, or inaccurate expenditures being paid resulting from weaknesses in the review and analysis of claims	Heightened opportunities for fraud resulting in potential loss of project funds; potential threat to subsequent maintenance or warranty claims

Source: Office of Anticorruption and Integrity, Asian Development Bank.

APPENDIX List of Proactive Integrity Reviews of Health Projects

Country	Project	PIR Report Issuance Date
Bangladesh	Second Urban Primary Health Care Project	Dec 2012
Indonesia	Decentralized Health Services I Project	Dec 2005
Lao People's Democratic Republic	Second Greater Mekong Subregion Regional Communicable Diseases Control Project	Dec 2013
Mongolia	Fifth Health Sector Development Project	Aug 2017 Jan 2019 (follow-up)
Mongolia	Second Health Sector Development Project	Dec 2008
Mongolia	Third Health Sector Development Project	Jan 2010
Philippines	Credit for Better Health Care Project	Jul 2015

PIR = proactive integrity review.

Note: Full PIR reports started to be published only in 2008. PIR reports prior to 2008 published on the Asian Development Bank (ADB) website only contain report abstracts/summaries.

Source: Office of Anticorruption and Integrity, Asian Development Bank.

www.ingramcontent.com/pod-product-compliance
Lightning Source LLC
Chambersburg PA
CBHW050058220326
41599CB00045B/7467